Grandpa Saba Bear Saves the Sun

He-he-he!

He-he-he!

He-he-he!

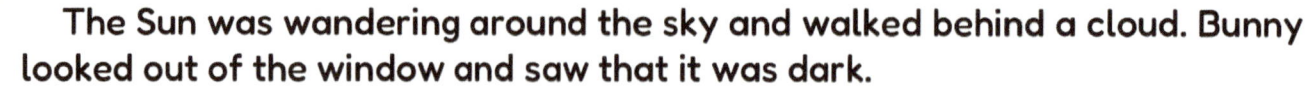

The Sun was wandering around the sky and walked behind a cloud. Bunny looked out of the window and saw that it was dark.

Magpies also saw that it was dark and, hopping over fields, screeched: "Disaster! Disaster! The Crocodile swallowed the Sun in the sky!"

They knew that only the Crocodile, a famous villain, could do such a thing.

Baba's and Saba's House

The Bears

Darkness spread everywhere: nobody could go out for fear of getting lost.

The gray sparrow cried: "Oh, dear Sun, please come out. Life is so hard without you: we cannot find food in the dark."

Bunnies on the lawn cried too: they got lost and could not find their way back home.

After several hours of darkness, two rams knocked on the central gate of the animal community. They called: "Hey, animals, come out. You must defeat the Crocodile, so that this selfish brute, who thinks only of his own good, let the Sun out into the sky again!"

But the furry citizens were cautious. "How can we challenge the Crocodile? He is ferocious and full of teeth, and he surely would not return the Sun to us."

So, they ran to the Bear's den, saying: "It's time for you, Bear, to sacrifice your personal comfort to the common welfare and go save the Sun."

The Bear did not like to fight, he was a grandfather.

His grand-cubs called him Grandpa Saba because his full name was Saba Bear – first name Saba and family name Bear.

Exactly at that time he was going around a large swampy patch in his backyard, searching for the cubs, growling piteously: "Where have you disappeared, why have you run away from me?" He could not see them because it was so dark.

Grandma Bear (whom her grand-cubs called Baba) was searching the wood around the yard, turning every tree trunk and looking under it for her lost grandkids. She was very worried and mumbled to herself distractedly: "Where, where are you? Did somebody hurt you?" She was walking all day long, not finding a single cub, while owls stared at her with their unseeing eyes.

Mama Rabbit came to the Bear and said: "This piteous growling does not help anyone. Instead, go and claw the Crocodile with your mighty claws, tear him apart, if need be, tear the Sun out of his jaws, and when it again shines in the sky, your furry ball grandkids, your chubby bear cubs, will come home on their own and say: "Hello, Grandpa, here we are!"

Then the Bear rose and growled loudly but not piteosly and ran to the Big River.

In the Big River lay the Crocodile and one could see fire burning in his mouth. But it was not fire – it was the bright stolen sun.

The Bear approached the Crocodile quietly and touched his shoulder. "Listen," he said, "Spit out the Sun. Otherwise, I'll have to wrestle it from you and might break your bones. This would teach you not to steal our Sun. The whole world is upset and you don't care!"

The Crocodile only laughed: "He-he-he. If I wanted, I could swallow the Moon too."

This irritated the Bear. "You, impudent reptile!" he snarled, jumped on the Crocodile, and forcibly opened his jaw.

The Crocodile yelped and his many sharp teeth released the Sun, which fell out of his mouth and rolled back onto the sky.

Immediately its light glimmered on the water and twinkled in the bushes, and the whole world sparkled and glistened and glowed.

Birds began flying after insects, and bunnies on the lawn jumped and performed summersaults.

And lo and behold: bear cubs, like happy kittens, traipsed on their chubby feet straight to their furry Gramps: "Hello, Grandpa Saba, here we are!"

All the bunnies and squirrels and boys and girls were happy. They hugged and kissed the old Bear and thanked him for bringing the Sun back to them.

Letter to Parents and Teachers of Little Kids

It is difficult to find books that can help little children to choose what they want to be when they grow up. With so many grownups around them struggling with their identities, with so many choices, and so little knowledge, preschoolers today need such help. To develop their selves and decide who they are, they need simple, non-confrontational ideals. That's why, after decades of study and writing about our complex society, which makes identity-formation so problematic, I decided to create a series of books for very young children.

"Miss Buzzz, the Fly" and the four stories following it: "Doctor Hurtz," "The Giant Cockroach," "Topsy-Turvy," and "Grandpa Saba Bear Saves the Sun" are prose stories adapted from the rhymed tales in Russian by Korney Chukovsky, a great children's literature writer and student of child psychology, written about a hundred years ago.

For generations these stories provided a moral compass to little Russians, Ukrainians, Georgians, Kazakh, and others, often forced to grow up in confusing and scary times. Now, as we, too, are caught up in confusing and scary times, they may be particularly helpful for little Americans and other English-speakers. Chukovsky's goal in writing was to teach a child **how to be a good person, above all else,** to cultivate in the child kindness (humane disposition) and empathy, "this marvelous ability to worry about other people's misfortunes, to rejoice at other people's joys, and to experience another person's destiny as one's own." A good person would focus on others, not on oneself, and have courage to help the helpless and defend the defenseless whenever such help and defense could be needed. A truly bad person, in distinction, would be someone who intentionally hurt someone else. There are wonderful role models for children in Chukovsky's stories: from a dashing brave mosquito, who saves a hapless fly from the clutches of a cruel spider to a selfless veterinarian Dr. Hurtz, who crosses the world to cure little animals in a far-off corner from numerous childhood diseases. The child learns that anyone can be a good person, no matter whether one has six legs, four legs, two legs, or no legs at all.

And there are also models of what one should not be: cowardly animals, believing rumors about and hiding from a giant cockroach, who turns on inspection to be a regular insect on skinny legs and, as such, eaten by a sparrow; insects, thinking only about their own safety and abandoning Miss Buzzz, whose friends they pretended to be in good times, in her hour of need; silly kittens who decide on a whim to oink like piglets and set the blue sea on fire, or selfish folk, who would not move a claw or a hoof to save the sun from the Crocodile who stole it, but expect the old grandfather Bear to do this for them. Why? **Because grandparents would do anything to make the world better for their grandchildren.**

www.ingramcontent.com/pod-product-compliance
Lightning Source LLC
Chambersburg PA
CBHW050750110526
44591CB00002B/34